THE PURPOSE FOR THE PAIN

HEALED ❈ DELIVERED ❈ SET-FREE ❈ RESTORED

THE PURPOSE FOR THE PAIN

HEALED ❈ DELIVERED ❈ SET-FREE ❈ RESTORED

Min. Sonja Pinckney Rhodes

For information on the content of this book, email:
JMPinckneyPublishing@gmail.com

JMPinckney Publishing, LLC
Goose Creek, SC 29445

Printed in the United States of America

ISBN: 979-8-9865984-7-5

CONTENTS

PREFACE

In preparation of writing this book, The Purpose for the Pain, I sought God...period. I knew in my spirit that another book would be birthed almost immediately after the first book; however, I waited on God before I penned the first sentence. When the title was spoken into my spirit, I could only see, feel and imagine what it would entail. God is moving mightily in my life and at times, I am overwhelmed, I feel inadequate and to be truthful, afraid that the assignment is too big. In actuality, it is but with the help of the Holy Spirit, we can do all things through Him who strengthens us.

Pastor Emeritus Augustus D. Robinson gave me the scripture Isaiah 40:32 when I was going through a tough time dealing with the abandonment of my ex-husband. His instructions were to read and meditate on it for 7 days straight and I was obedient to the directive. I truly didn't understand at the time, but as time and years went by, I could see the manifestations of God working in and through my life. Doors began to open that I did not touch, blessings began to flow like streams of living water and favor followed/follows me. I am not only growing in the knowledge of Jesus Christ, but He allows me the opportunity to be a blessing to so many… but it's only by and through the grace of God that I am able to do any and all things.

Today, I share of God's goodness and His amazing grace that others may come to know Jesus for themselves. The Apostle Paul said, Brethren, I count not myself to have apprehended: but *this* one thing *I do*, forgetting those things which are behind, and reaching forth unto those things which are before me. As I trusted God more, I yearned to draw closer to Him. I wanted to *know* Him, and the power of his resurrection for myself. Accepting my call to ministry to proclaim the gospel of Jesus Christ of Nazareth, was a new beginning; however, I still felt a call to go deeper. I never wanted to go back to school, although my Father, the late Dea. Johnny Pinckney, often encouraged me not to stop short, I adamantly rejected the idea. He was planting. Consequently, I just couldn't shake this feeling and when my Pastor, Dr. Byron L. Benton, declared it, it resonated in my spirit. Therefore, I started Seminary in March of 2022 and it has been an amazing journey of taking me deeper unto deep. As I continue on this journey of faith, my purposes will be fulfilled as I follow Christ, to encourage others that He has a great plan for their lives to prosper them in all their ways. We may have to cry sometimes, but trust that God works all things out for the good of them who love Him. He is able to do all things, but fail.

Letter from Mother, Mrs. Mary Pinckney

Words of Wisdom to My Amazing Daughter: Minister Sonja Pinckney Rhodes

To my elder daughter, Sonja Rene Pinckney Rhodes, I am very proud to be your Mother and I am proud of you and all of your accomplishments! Life can be a journey filled with many challenges, and I have seen how God has blessed you to go through all with and by His grace. I want you to continue to learn to trust your feelings, your convictions and most of all to trust God knowing that He will never leave you, to hold on to your strong belief in God who will always lead you in the right direction; to be strong, courageous and be bold in what you believe, because the Lord thy God is with you wherever you go and no weapon, word, distraction, doubt or fear will ever prosper because you belong to the Almighty God. I have always told you that you have the favor of God. His hand is upon you to accomplish everything that He has purposed for your life.

Sonja, you have always had a sweet spirit. Guard your heart and always show love and humility in all things. God has blessed you to receive honors and recognition for the great work He has done and is doing in your life, so hold on to His hand and follow His voice that will always lead you to be prosperous, because you are an overcomer and a survivor. The blessings that God has given to you, remember to show the same honor and recognition to others that He places in your path. Also, know that true friendship is so hard to find, but always show the same kindness to others that God has shown to you and don't let anyone take the gift of your sweet spirit that God has given you away... the world didn't give it and the world can't take it away.

Dignity and Honor are yours, because God ordained it to be so, He sanctified you to be set apart and different, so wear it, walk in it and be proud of the woman He has created in His likeness. Through all of your accomplishments, you have remained humble and God has so much more in store for you. Have confidence in yourself and confidence in God that the good work He has started, He will complete in you; for there's a great future that awaits you.

From the beginning, you were special. Watching you grow into a beautiful young lady has blessed my life, and for everything that you are, and everything that you do, my heart is filled with Love for you. I am so very proud of you every day of my life and your father's life as it was, because you are fearfully strong, wonderfully created in love and beautifully made by the hands of God!

Love Always and Forever,
Your Mother, Mary Pinckney

Pastor Emeritus Augustus D. Robinson, Jr.
Mt. Moriah Missionary Baptist Church

A TESTIMONIAL REFLECTION OF GOD'S
ANOINTING UPON THE LIFE AND MINISTRY
OF MINISTER SONJA PINCKNEY RHODES

It is always a unique and aspiring blessing to be given an opportunity by God to witness the Power of His Word in action as He makes and mold His handy work in His Hand. (Philippians 1:6) Many years ago, as the Pastor of Mt. Moriah Missionary Baptist Church, I was granted the joy of The Lord to become an instrument of God's transforming Power by being granted the privilege of discipling and becoming the planter and waterer of many who were seeking their destiny for our Savior Jesus Christ. One of those roses that I was entrusted to care and nurture in the Faith was my spiritual daughter, Sonja Pinckney Rhodes. I was granted by God, along with other spiritual leaders to accompany Sonja on, and through her journey of pain, disappointment, discouragement, doubt, on her attaining her victory through

Jesus Christ. Even though having gotten wounded by the adversary, Sonja maintained her focus and grip on Jesus Christ and His powerful hand. Yes, we have witnessed her spiritual growth as she has risen from the pit on her darkest journey to God's mountain top of success. Sonja is a living testimony of how the power of God, through Jesus Christ, can resurrect his children from being victims, to becoming Overcoming Victors! As a testimony of her victories over depression, and physical and mental abuse, she has answered her call to the Ministry of The Gospel of Jesus Christ, became a certified counselor and advocate for abused women prevention, an aspiring Christian author of more than three (3) transforming and inspirational books, became a licensed Realtor and has received the additional favor of God to establish and become the owner of her publishing company, JMPinckney Publishing of books, and journals. What a Mighty God, and Savior we serve!! In closing, I insert the words of the great apostle Paul in his letter to the church at Corinth.

In (I Corinthians 3:6-7)
6. Paul says I planted, Apollos watered, but God gave the increase.
7. So then neither he who plants is anything, nor he who waters, but God who gives the increase. (NKJV)

Rev. Dr. A. D. Robinson Jr. D.D
Pastor Emeritus

FOREWORD WRITTEN BY REVEREND GLORIA LIGHTFOOT

The Purpose for the Pain is an experience of how God can deliver through perseverance of abuse, neglect, failure, rejection and insults. Having purpose propelled Ms. Pinckney Rhodes to trust God and to press her way, by hoping in God. God is a lamp unto her feet and the light unto her path. Because of God's word, she is destined for greatness. The Prophet Jeremiah reminds us that God foreknew, sanctified and ordained us before we came forth out of the womb; therefore He already knows the plans for our lives, to be prosperous, that no harm may come to us and to give us a hope and a future. She thanks God for the Esther anointing that has strategically positioned her by God to set her in a place of influence. She is a mighty paradigm of how God can use anyone. The physical and spiritual preparation she endured aligned her to answer God's call that purposed her for destiny. Walking by faith is definitely a way of life, as God has blessed Sonja in the past and brought her out of the miry clay. Every time she turns around, God continues to bless her over and over again. She has stood on His promises that He will never leave her nor will He forsake her. It's evident that her trials and tribulations have proven God's faithfulness to her as she overcame obstacles in her life for such a time as this to proclaim the goodness of the Lord in the land of the living.

The enemy brings adversity to keep us in bondage from reaching our divine destiny that God has ordained for us. In her lifetime, she may have faced devastating times of uncertainty in the world, but through it all, the Lord has protected and guarded her from all harm and danger. The Purpose for the Pain is a testimonial of experiences to help build courage, confidence, faith, and hope in God, knowing that with Him all things are possible. The affirmations penned by Sonja Pinckney Rhodes will not only center your mind and spirit, but it also grants you the strength necessary to face any challenge that may arise. How we view our relationship with ourselves starts with a simple belief in who we are and what we can become. Positive thinking channels our energies that allow us to focus on developing stronger mindsets that awaken the inner truths we often forget. As you will determine, Ms. Sonja has sought a closer relationship with the Lord. Through her stories and illustrations, the reader will be inspired with a renewed sense of the light the Lord shines through her in the midst of life's challenges. As often stated, our past does not determine our future. Prior mistakes, disappointments, and struggles can be used to help build our character and overcome obstacles to become the women of God that He has intended for each of us. We all face trials and tribulations but that should not cause us to lose heart. A women motivated by purpose remains focused and faithful until God transforms her life to be who He has ordained her to become in His Kingdom. They remain encouraged knowing that God will give them beauty for ashes because of their faith in God, and that they are more than conquerors through the purpose of Christ Jesus' love for them.

May you be blessed through the powerful affirmations of God's divine purpose that is displayed through the declarations in this inspiring book.

ACKNOWLEDGMENTS

I am nothing, nothing, nothing at all without my Lord, and Savior, Jesus the Christ of Nazareth. I thank Him for His goodness and His amazing grace that has brought me out of darkness into His marvelous light. I was a wretch undone, living in a world of sin, then He reached way down, picked me up and turned me around. He allowed me to walk in the fullness of His grace by placing my feet on solid ground. To Him I owe my all; my everything. I thank God for this opportunity to breathe again.

To my awesome parents, the handsome and late Dea. Johnny Pinckney and my beautiful mother, Mary Pinckney, I thank God for being a great example of what parents should be. Taking us to church and introducing us to Christ is the best gift that a parent can give to their child. You not only took us, but you lived a Christian life and taught us the value of being grateful to God, instilling the importance of manners and that education is vitally important. Your love is what covered us while growing up in your household and into our adulthood. I now teach those same values to my children and grandchildren. Thank you for a life well-lived.

To my siblings, Jonathan (Andrea) Pinckney, Sherri Pinckney (Derrick) Kinloch, and bonus brother, Dennis (Sylvia) Michael. I have memories that no one else can ever claim or live up to. We shared some of the same experiences, meals, discipline (lol!), but most of all, the same love that was extended to us and among us. There were definitely great times and we also endured the sadness of our loved ones that are now our cloud of witnesses. Thank you for the unconditional love and I take joy in seeing your successes in life and even the joy of seeing our grandchildren play with each other. May our bond last forever and a day.

I thank God for a "special aunt" Rebecca Bennett, better known as Auntie Kay, who has always been there for me. She has always encouraged me, and have always listened to me when I faced obstacles in life. Besides my Mother, she slayed my hair for more than 30 years, as my stylist. I thank you for not judging but instead, showing love to me. Today, I enjoy taking you places and especially, shopping with you. I will always cherish every moment that we have shared.

To my awesome children that God has blessed me with, Jon (Markita) Pinckney, Sr., Andre' Christopher Rhodes, and grandchildren, Jon Jr., Ari and Nia Pinckney, you are my pride and joy. I am so very proud of each of you and I pray always that God blesses everything your hands touch and everywhere your feet trod. May the blessing of God overflow and overshadow you all the days of your lives. May He be a fence all around you every day, protecting you from the enemy who walks about like a roaring lion seeking whom he may devour. May there be peace that surpasses all understanding that will guard your hearts and your minds, in Christ Jesus.

Thank you to everyone: Senior Pastor Byron L. Benton, Pastor Emeritus, Augustus D. Robinson, Jr., Deacon Jervey & Gloria Smalls, Dea. Emeritus and Dea. Major & Rev. Gloria Lightfoot, Denna Nell, Nancy LaRoche, Chairman Dea. & Deas. Thomas and Simone Withers, Adrian Gadsden, Min. Ranese Harrell, Min. Geraldine Williams, Rev. Tony Jennings, Rev. Patricia Crawford, Betty McKelvey, Ethel Maxey Garner, Dea. Charles Maxey, Aunt Charlie Williams, Aunt Auto Lee Smalls, Deas. Richardine Edwards, Min. & Mrs. Tristan & Tirese Simmons, Dea. & Deas. DeShean & LaTasha Garrett, Dana Price Richardson, Dea. & Deas. Henry and Karen Middleton, Shanel Burwell, Dea. Emeritus & Deas. John and Renee Matthews, and so many more. Please know that I love and appreciate you all. I am blessed to have a strong and loving community.

CHAPTER ONE

As we know, the heart has four chambers; two upper and two lower. They each function independently to accomplish and maintain the normal flow of its purpose. Their jobs are to receive incoming blood in the upper chamber and for the lower to pump blood out of the heart. It is said that too much of anything is not good for us; therefore, everything is to be done in moderation. Our purposes in life are synonymous to how the heart functions; in fact, the heart of the matter is that everything centers on the matters of the heart. Instinctively, we are drawn to our natural heart; however, if we make Jesus our choice, He becomes the center of our joy, our lives, our businesses, and relationships; actually, our everything. As life throw curve balls and we get knocked off our high horses a time or two; we begin to learn the cycle of life. We fall down, but we get up or as the Proverbs says it, a just man that falls seven times, gets back up. Whatever happens in life, it's only by the grace of God that we are healed, delivered, set-free and restored. He is our heart regulator.

As we seek Him to create in us a clean heart, He will also renew a right spirit within us. Speaking of the heart again and it's functionalities, a good man out of the good treasure of his heart brings forth that which is good; and an evil man out of the evil treasure of his heart brings forth that which is evil: for out of the abundance of the heart, the mouth speaks (Luke 6:45). Simply, what goes in must come out. Jesus is reminding us in this passage that our speech and actions reveal our real, underlying beliefs, attitudes, and motivations. The good impressions we try to make cannot last if our heart is deceptive. What is in your heart will come out in your speech and behavior.

Don't lose hope when you fall short, as we all fall short of God's glory. Don't be discouraged when people falsely accuse, disregard or ostracize you. The dirty, muddy waters may sometimes blur our vision from seeing the true essence of the light that surrounds our very being. Hold fast to God's unchanging hands, as sung so profoundly by the Chicago Mass Choir, because time is filled with swift transitions. Moreover, it is in those dark and shallow moments that we are becoming... becoming a new creature, becoming stronger, becoming informed, becoming the person that God has ordained for us to be-come. As I wander through the valley of the shadows of discouragement or hopelessness with someone in this moment, I encourage you to walk in blind faith knowing that you are not alone. One of the promises of God is that He will go before you and will be with you; he will never leave you nor will He forsake us. Do not be afraid; do not be discouraged. He is as close as the air we breathe and He comforts us in His loving arms. It's in moments of despair when we feel the pressures of life and the torment of oppression of knees on our backs, necks and chest. Life happens and it's real. Don't be deceived by the enemy disguised as your friend, confidant, lover, sister or brother. He comes to kill, steal and to destroy you and your anointing. Pray for God to increase your discernment then watch how He changes things. You will begin to see the devil prey on you in the midst of your troubled situations, but also in your most triumphant moments. The prey of the terrible shall be delivered: for God will contend with him who contends with you, and He will save His children by proving to the world that He is God by doing the impossible. He will make your enemy your footstool causing the captor to set his captives free and then helping them leave. Never should you doubt that God will fulfill his promises. He will even do the impossible to make them come true.

As I reflect on my first book, From Pain to Purpose, I didn't realize I was still being held captive, until I began to write. Although it was difficult to experience the feelings of abandonment when my ex-husband departed, God was making ways out of no way for my children and me. The captor was gone but my heart was still in bondage. I continued to live oppressed until my spiritual eyes were opened to envision the evidence of the manifestation living inside of me. I could only then see how I remained in that state of mind, which allowed the same type of spirit to come into my space. It was another hard lesson to learn that I should not put confidence in man or by trusting the flesh by their fulfillment of duties or level of human activity. I was beginning to draw strength, inspiration, and support from various individuals, such as my family, church community, within myself and from God. Our confidence should always be in our internal faith to God, because He values the attitude of our heart above all else. Philippians reminds us to beware of dogs, beware of evil workers, beware of the concision and I will add to beware of the kiss of Judas. Most of all stand firm on the word of God to lead, guide, protect and to bless you. Trust in the Almighty God that the setback will be your setup for your comeback. I rest on the ultimate God will make a way scripture: "Behold, I am doing a new thing; now it springs forth, do you not perceive it? I will make a way in the wilderness and rivers in the desert" (Isa. 43:19).

I have felt the sting of sexual violation by my schizophrenic paternal uncle, a beautiful grandmother who discriminated against me because of the dark color/pigmentation of my skin, rejected in school because of my thin body frame, the embarrassment of teenage pregnancy, and two failed/abusive marriages, just to name a few. It seems like a lifetime of heartache and disappointment, right? Someone once said, "Expectation is the root of all heartache." The quote acknowledges that when we encounter disappointment, our hopes and expectations are out of line with reality. However, all of my trials, all of my troubles, all of my silent tears were obstacle courses to strengthen my physical body, emotional mind, and spiritual being to prepare me for the plan that God has for me. See, trials come to make us strong. Nehemiah said, the joy of the Lord is my strength. In the midst of my turmoil,

I lost my appetite and my zeal for my God-given purposes. I was struggling to maintain my appearance among my peers and family. However, there was a fight inside of me and although the enemy was coming in like a flood, and as he thought he had stripped me of my dignity and self-esteem, the Holy Spirit was speaking to my spirit in the mid-night hour to give me peaceful rest for my body, my mind and my spirit. If God is for you, who can be against you (Rom. 8:31)? He was providing the resources that were required to feed my children and myself, and He gave me the tools, as a faithful worshipper to keep my mind on Him that He would keep me in perfect peace. I may have lost some things, but I didn't lose hope. God is continuously working in my life as I grow in His grace and unconditional love. Nothing else could have prepared me for such a time as this. We serve a God who works out everything in conformity with the purpose of His will (Eph. 1:11). God uses us to fulfill His purposes. No matter what my situation or circumstances were, God's instruments of deliverance and victory had my name assigned to it. "For such a time as this," God prepared me to be brave, committed and obedient to step out in faith and accomplish His work. I am not here by accident! I am eternally grateful to God for sustaining, protecting, and keeping my mind in perfect peace. The bible says that our trials come to make us strong and that we should rejoice in our suffering. I say to you, in addition to that, keep holding on to God's unchanging hands, don't lose hope, don't look back with regret because weeping truly endures for a night and your joy will surely come in the morning. Trust the process and know that God's eternal promise is that He will never leave you nor will He forsake you. Let me break it down and make it clear for you; He will never send you back, let go of you, relax on you, place you on hold, send you to voicemail, loosen His grip on you, or give up on you.

CHAPTER TWO

Life has had its ups and downs and time is filled with swift transitions. What does that mean? Life changes quickly and the effects of the rain, the storm, the disappointments, and sadness unloads express packages at each of our front doors and in the cavities of our hearts. Change is uncomfortable, but it's necessary for the maturity of growing in Christ. In times of change, we may become fearful, anxious or discouraged because we are unsure of what is going to happen or how everything will unfold. However, we can rest in the truth found in Jeremiah 29:11 knowing that God does have a plan for us and that He will lead us on the right path when we place our trust in Him. Paul said it best when he testified of being contented in whatever state of mind or life he was in. I believe he is saying that we have to know how to be satisfied when we are in lack or in abundance. The secret is to draw upon Christ's power and His promises for strength to help you to be contented. He will supply all of your needs, but in a way that He knows what's best for you. When we are contented, we can see life from God's point of view by focusing on what we're designed to do and not what we feel we should have to do. Setting our priorities in order and being grateful for everything God has given us, detaches us from the non-essentials to concentrate on the eternal. Often, the desire for more or better possessions is really a longing to fill an empty space in our lives. However, the answer lies in our perspectives, our priorities, and our source of power if we seek ye first His kingdom and righteousness that all these things will be added to you (Matt. 6:33).

Although, I love Paul and his tenacity to stick with his beliefs, especially after the scales were removed from his eyes, Joseph is also my guy. He was intelligent, patient, strong and good looking. He was also gracious to his brothers who betrayed him. This brother knew, understood and discerned the Lord's voice through visions and dreams. He didn't necessarily dream the dream at all times, but he also interpreted the dreams of others. He allowed the Lord to order his steps and he had the courage to run when he was faced with temptation. He knew his gift was from God, but he respected the Gifter of the gift, even the more. It's difficult to wait on God when we just don't understand the rhyme or reason of our circumstances. But, when we need deliverance, when we need a little more faith, when we need to stand still, and see the salvation of the Lord, He will do great and mighty things in and through us, as He did when He saved Israel out of the hand of the Egyptians. The blessing is not necessarily for us but to be a blessing and a testament of the goodness of Jesus to the world. Job 13:15 says, "Though he slay me, yet will I trust him. If we look at all of the seasons that take place in the earth, they are reflective of all the seasons we go through in our lives; winter, spring, summer, fall. Everybody loves spring, when everything is blossoming and blooming. It conveys feelings of increased energy, happiness or of amorousness. Others have a tendency to look forward to the warmth of summer when things are bright, cheery and uplifting. People find themselves enamored in fall when things are changing. They may feel a mix of nostalgic yearning, renewed optimism, and abstract melancholy. It's hard to find people who like winter, but think it's rooted in the way that while there is winter in your life, spring is still coming. We trust God even when we don't like what life is serving, and we trust Him even when we're at the crossroads of life trying to figure out if this is God or the enemy? God is worth the wait. It may be demanding to do, disconcerting to comprehend or difficult to hold onto Him, but I challenge you to have the faith of Job. In the face of all your adversarial conditions, resolve in yourself that though he slay me, yet still will I trust Him!

As we begin to understand our assignments and the challenges it may bring, we begin to realize that it always includes others. The book of Genesis tells us to be fruitful and multiply. In other words, God wants families to grow so that the gift is passed on to others that they may learn of His spiritual fruits, develop His character and testify of His goodness and of His amazing grace. God granted me the gift of two handsome and successful sons, Jon Michael Pinckney and Andre' Christopher Rhodes. They are ten years apart. The pride and joy of hearing their cry and holding them for the first time was a love that cannot be described or vastly understood in the finite mind.

...how we use our tongue, determines if we are giving life to others or killing their spirits with our words.

God allowed a seed to be planted, developed, and nurtured, as my body went through the metamorphosis stages of child birth. During this process many questions and doubts went through my mind: what will I look like in the midst of this transition, will I be able to carry full term, how can I push through this; how do I protect, care for and provide and will my babies be healthy? These were common and real life questions. Like giving birth to a newborn baby, the pain that we experience is necessary for new life to be born. Although, there are ten years between the birth of my sons, and the pain was nearly unbearable, I had forgotten what it felt like. Therefore, I questioned the how's, what's and when's of this miraculous occurrence of bearing a child once again. This is sometimes how life reminds us that we will have difficulties, hurts, pains, and how we will have to struggle at times to make way for new life, new hope and new joy that often comes out of the most painful and embarrassing situations. In the end result, we should come to the realization that what we experience is for a greater purpose. Life gives life and as the bible says, life and death are in the power of the tongue. Therefore, how we use our tongue, determines if we are giving life to others or killing their spirits with our words. It's a taught and learned behavior and sometimes it's the only bible people may see; through our life living and interactions. Let love always lead you even through the most intricate moments in your life, as it give life to others. We are not our own, but conduits for the Living Water to overflow into the lives of others, that they may be fruitful and multiply, enabling them to do what God has commanded; to feed His sheep.

CHAPTER THREE

In my first book, *From Pain to Purpose: A Bridge Over Troubled Waters*, I disclosed information of destructive secrets that tormented me most of my life. I never knew the domino influence it caused by covering up the violations and not confronting the issues until my heart's chambers began to malfunction because of the dysfunction caused by the influx of sadness, shame and grief. My heart was broken and I had lost my sense of direction and found myself wallowing in muddy waters. In my moment of despair, I cried out to the Lord and began to fight the good fight of faith...in the midst of my desolation. Somehow, it became a way of life; the norm. Through the storms of life and through the rains, I prayed, read my bible, attended church services and became involved in various ministries to fill the voids in my life and to center my thoughts on the One who turned me around, and pulled me out of the miry clay. The light was beginning to shine again; unspeakable joy and laughter were in my bones. I was excited about the smell of the sweet aroma of healing that stimulated every desire that danced within me. Growing pains were drooling with the taste of victory. The harder the pitcher threw curve balls, the more precise I became when I fired the homerun with the power of the word of God over my life's circumstances. Meditating on God's continued promises that I can do all things through Him who strengthens me; no weapon formed against me shall prosper; I am fearfully and wonderfully made and that He loves me so much that no one or nothing can dare snatch me out of the palm of His hands, resonated deeply within my soul.

I learned how to give voice to the illusions of fear. I learned that secrets are detrimental to spiritual growth. It's mind-blowing the reality of the bondage or enslavement that I was to the unwarranted, unprovoked and unjustifiable touching, lies, deceit, and slanderous secrets that were buried inside the core of my very being. If we're not careful, its roots will begin to take form and attach itself to the life line agents in our minds, bodies and spirits to stunt our spiritual growth. Before you know it, you may find yourself a victim to the deadly schematics of your adversary the devil who walks about like a roaring lion seeking whom He may devour (I Pet. 5:8). But! There is a voice that is attached to everything that happens in our lives. Some are deliberate by you and sometimes by others. However, His sheep hears His voice and He know them, and they follow Him. Meaning, they will obey the voice of the Lord. They will take heed to His voice. They will not turn to the left nor to the right when He has spoken. It is imperative to understand who God is, so that the true gospel of Jesus Christ is proclaimed without limitations or imperfections. Positioning complete confidence in God and making the decision of whom you will serve is the general basis to grow in ministry and to serve the true and living God. When I released the fear of people, my eyes were opened and I became increasingly thirsty for the true and living water.

The more intensely I sought the Lord to win His approval and not the approval of man, it became evident that it was the only way of breaking the walls of inferiority that is vital to proclaiming the unadulterated (pure) gospel of Jesus Christ. However, it was birthed from a place of brokenness. God was my solid rock during my time of despair. He had already ordained and sanctified me according to His plans; therefore, the pain was for a purpose and a desired outcome. However, that outcome could only be realized by knowing the true essence of God. Letting go of insecurities will liberate and unshackle the chains and bondage from the heavy burdens of life. Releasing fears that places limitations on our gifts allow us to know more profoundly who God is in our lives. One of the objectives is to realize that our freedom came with a price that was already paid by Christ on the cross at Calvary. Belief in His birth, sacrifice, death, burial; resurrection and ascension, love and saving power is the summation of our faith. Knowing God as our Savior, Redeemer, Master and King validates that we are relevant and not here by accident. The period in my life when I hid behind the mask, I believed that it covered and protected me; however, it was only by the power of His resurrection that I was sheltered from the storm, raised from hopelessness and restored unto joy. His love sustained me, His power raised me, and His compassion strengthened me by breaking the yoke of bondage that set me free. It is important to make a decision of whom we should serve. But as for me and my house, we will serve the Lord (Jos. 24:15), God Almighty, Ruler of everything and King of all kings.

CHAPTER FOUR

It is the will of God who ordains our paths and our purposes. We are here on this earth to worship and serve God and to follow the leading and the guiding of the Holy Spirit. God knows all of our short-comings, our insecurities, our weaknesses and our fears because He created us. He is not concerned about our inadequacies, because we are to depend on and trust Him solely and completely to direct our every step. The bible says that "obedience is better than sacrifice" (I Sam. 15:22); therefore, apart from what is pleasing to God, only an obedient disposition of mind is in itself something good. A disobedient disposition has no moral value and can be summed up to be rebellious or defiant self-dependence. As I look back over my life, I can see how I have allowed fear to hinder my walk with God by muzzling my voice to speak up in many situations. As the Apostle Paul told Timothy, "God has not given us the spirit of fear," (2 Tim 1:7) or of cowardice. He has empowered us to overcome our weaknesses. There is no time for fearfulness or timidity in the Kingdom of God. Any opportunity that presents itself to share the gospel of Jesus Christ and His saving grace, should be an opportunity to witness of His love and power to help transform, heal, deliver, set-free or restore from the yoke of bondage. And as I witness to others, it encourages my soul to continue on my journey for Christ as I continue to take a fearless and moral inventory of self, use every message God gives for a self examination, and let God determine my role in the proclamation process and provision in this ministry in which I was called. Nonetheless, staying self-centered will keep the doors open to carry around the feelings of unworthiness, and feelings of inadequacy. And as a side note, God is not concerned about our feelings because emotions waver; therefore, it's not rooted or grounded on any just cause. It feels what it feels and is moved by whatever or whomever disturbs the comfort and convenience of staying safe within our own personal bubble of self-centeredness, self-absorption, and self-awareness. It also has a tendency of creating a numbing effect when it comes to the needs and cares of others; unless it is for personal gain or recognition. Feelings cannot be trusted, is not reliable or even steadfast.

Cultivating a genuine relationship with God creates a better understanding of who He is, which authenticates the knowledge that his approval is all that we will ever need. He is the great I Am. He is everything we need, every breath we take, every move we make, every answer to every question; our provider, protector, healer, deliverer, He's our Master, Messiah and Savior!

Consequently, establishing a personal relationship with God is vital to proclaiming the gospel and for knowing who we are and whose we are. Cultivating a genuine relationship with God creates a better understanding of who He is, which authenticates the knowledge that his approval is all that we will ever need. He is the great I Am. He is everything we need, every breath we take, every move we make, every answer to every question; our provider, protector, healer, deliverer, He's our Master, Messiah and Savior! When He speak directly to me and I make the conscience decision to move according to His directive, working out my salvation with fear and trembling, there's a certain level of spiritual confidence that overtakes me and confirms that I am more than enough in and through Him. I have found that making Jesus my "first" choice is an on-going process, like the infinite sign. It has no ending, and like "climbing Jacob's ladder, every rung goes higher and higher. In light, we instinctively assume that our faith is about ascending. Explicitly, transformation must take place to faithfully and authentically proclaim the true gospel of Jesus Christ. It is necessary to take hold of the scope of God's love that He gave His only begotten Son to save our souls from the doom and the pits of hell. He came that we may have life and to have it in abundance that we may be filled with the power of His resurrection. We are commanded to go! Go into the entire world teaching all nations and baptizing them in the name of the Father, Son and Holy Spirit (Matt. 28: 19). The Great Commission tells us to go! It doesn't highlight the disposition of life's challenges, because we are purposed to spread the gospel in and out of season; when it feels good or not so good. When we are weak, He is strong and it's in the valley that we grow. Through my darkness, my fears and inadequacies that I still encounter as an adult, God gave me and has instilled in me the mindset to continue to press on to the mark of the high calling in Christ Jesus. See, it doesn't matter how nice you are to people, how much you study to show yourself approved unto God, what you look like, there will be people you will have to walk away from. As you grow in the grace of God, everyone will not be able to go with you. It was hurtful at first, but God began to show me through the power of discernment that they were not for me; nor were they for what I was for. Bishop Thomas Dexter Jakes explains it this way:

1. YOUR CONFIDANTS.

These are the people who ARE REALLY INTO YOU. They are for you. They weep when you weep and laugh when you laugh. They always listen to your problems and have time to rejoice with you. Nothing on earth can stop them from finding time for you. They are the ones you can keep secrets with. Your secrets, either good or bad are safe with them. They are to you what Jonathan was to David.

These kind of people are few, and if you have only three, what a blessed person you are!

2. YOUR CONSTITUENTS

These are the people WHO ARE FOR WHAT YOU ARE FOR. They are not for you, but for what you are called to do. They have no interest in your secrets. They have no time to either laugh or weep with you. They will go to any length to invest in your dream. They will put up adverts for you asking other investors to join them in supporting you. And once they are through with actualizing your dreams for you they will exit.

Your duty is to work with them, and if you make the mistake of taking them as your confidants, perhaps complain about a problem you are facing they will walk away from you and never look back.

They are not your "Jonathan". They are not your confidants. They are your constituents.

3. YOUR COMRADES

These are people WHO ARE AGAINST WHAT YOU ARE AGAINST. They are your fighters. They fight with you against your enemies. War gets them excited and they will never leave until they annihilate your foes.

The word of God says that we are not to put our trust in man because they will fail you every time. Some things are only accomplished by prayer and fasting. It is imperative to live a life of surrender to God. This is accomplished by examining our thoughts, refusing to fall into the temptations of sin and saying yes to righteousness, then submitting our ways to God's ways. The closer we get to Jesus, the more radical we become for Him. A true surrender is allowing Jesus to forgive our debts, and to release us from the bondage that we may be free to worship, free to serve and free to proclaim the gospel of Jesus Christ without fear or inadequacies.

CHAPTER FIVE

If we really want to know ourselves, it starts by first focusing on knowing God. It is my belief that it is the formula that helps us to live as we were meant to exist. Professor Wynand De Kock of Palmer Theological Seminary, philosophically expressed that, "To know God is to know yourself and to know yourself is to know God." Jeremiah, also known as the "weeping prophet" declares, "For I know the thoughts that I think toward you, saith the Lord, thoughts for peace, and not of evil, to give you an expected end" (Jer. 29: 11-13). Jeremiah was giving hope and he was warning the Israelites at the same time. Like Jeremiah, we should get to know God through our faithfulness to Him. When He gives us a word and challenges us to execute that word, we should never doubt but move with compassion, because we know Him and trust that He will provide, protect and deliver. Jeremiah wept because he was tender-hearted. He was dedicated to doing God's will regardless of what others said or who was against him. God's Word to His people in the day of

Jeremiah is still His sure word for us today. No mechanical gesture of knowing Him can procure the rich treasure that is more valuable than all gold. God's longing is that we all may look to Him that we may gain knowledge of who we are in Him. His arms are always open in loving invitation as we seek Him. It is just as true; however, that a diligent search is necessary for us to know Him. As we become conscious of His need, we sense the satisfying gift of God. Knowing Him is a sure answer for knowing ourselves if we seek Him with our whole heart or have a tender heart, as Jeremiah. For He is our creator; we are created in the image of Him in our moral, spiritual, and intellectual nature. His Spirit speaks to our spirit to know Him intimately and as we get to know Him, He will strengthen our lives and fill us with the hope of His glory.

In fact, one of the greatest desires of a Christian today is that men and women would know Christ. As I studied Kerygma in Theology my first semester, the main idea was to know God, to be known by God and to make God known that I may better proclaim the gospel of Jesus Christ. The bible affirms that **Moses** said to God, "I beseech thee, show me thy glory" (Exodus 33:18). Here, he is longing for God's abundance or an overflow of God. Moses could not see God's face and live, but he was permitted to stand on a rock while God's glory passed by to see an appearance of God. God was gracious to Moses and if we seek Him, He will be compassionate to us, as well. **David** said, "As the deer pants for the water brooks, so my soul pants for You, O God" (Psalm 42:1). This describes David as a man with God's spirit. He is born again, and His hunger and thirst is for the living God. Our inner longing for fellowship with God is in contrast with the intense craving of the deer as it wanders through the desert longing for the brooks. **Job** 14:14 says, "For I know that my redeemer lives." In Job's suffering, he had knowledge of the Lord to bring hope even in the midst of his greatest trials. Job's faith to see God in his flesh, even after his skin was destroyed, strongly implies that He knew God enough to heal him and to bring about a physical resurrection in his body and to restore him. **Paul** says that, "his heart belongs to God, to know Him is the power of the resurrection and the fellowship of His suffering" (Phil. 3:10). Paul is demonstrating that we should live our lives in such a way that the world knows that we are not of the world, because we have been called out of the world by a risen Savior. He is saying to know God is to gain practical day-by-day acquaintance with Him in such a way that we would become more Christ-like. Therefore, I tell you that the greatest desire of every true Christian is to know God. For every human objective centers on that one point, that if we know God, we would receive Him as Lord of our lives. At times, I felt alone and that I just didn't fit in, but it was in those moments that God was drawing me closer to Him. I didn't fit in, because He wanted me to be a cast-out with them that I may be casted-in with Him. I was never alone, as God's word proclaims that He is always with us and will never leave us nor forsake us. In the silence, God comforted me, encouraged my spirit, gave me peace and also strengthened me. Proverbs says to lean not to our own understanding and to trust Him in all His ways and He would direct our paths. I leaned on Isaiah scripture passage to wait on the Lord and to be of good courage and He would strengthen my heart and Psalm 27 that says, the Lord is my light and my salvation, whom shall I fear? He is the strength of my life, of whom shall I be afraid? There is a cliché that says, there is nothing to fear but fear itself (Franklin D. Roosevelt). God has not given us that spirit. He fills us with love, power and a sound mind (2 Tim. 1:7) and tells us not to fear men in their faces (Jer. 1:8). As long as our minds are stayed on Him, He will keep us in perfect peace. I am truly grateful that God has given me peace that surpasses all understanding that guards my heart and my mind!

The yearning and the urging that I feel is also a desire to know more of whom God is and His purpose for my life. I did not and still do not feel complete satisfaction, even as I grow in the knowledge of Jesus Christ. It is evident that the deeper I go, the deeper the calling to continually surrender my will for that of the Father's will is impacted upon me. This longing is becoming more and more confirmed in my spirit as Professor De Kock affirms this passion through his lectures that "it is an ongoing experience and calling to be in intimacy with our Lord and Savior Jesus Christ." I crave to feel His glory, not just in me but in those around me that my light may shine and others may see my good works, and glorify our Father in heaven (Matt 5:16). We are all meant to shine and manifest the glory of God and we all are ambassadors for Christ, created to do His good works (2 Cor. 5:20). Even through my feelings of inadequacy, verbal and physical abuse, and low self-esteem, God still had and has need of me to do His good works and for Him to be glorified. It is in times like these that we need a Savior who manifests Himself in the dark areas of our lives to show His power and authority in and through us. Jesus died to deliver us from the world, the bondage of corruptions and of death. The Holy Spirit lives within us to give us the power to overcome the world. This is a philosophical proclamation that if we are glorifying anything or anyone other than God, it is thus anti-Christian.

> The cross crucifies us to the world … when you die to the world, you turn away from the attractions and pleasures of the world; therefore, you become unattractive to the world … The point is this: as a minister of God, you must glory in the cross of Christ, not in yourself. God has given you everything in the cross of Christ, both life now and eternally – both deliverance from the lusts of this world and from the condemnation of the flesh, death, and judgment to come. Therefore, you must not seek worldly popularity and recognition, not seek to make a good impression nor to attract attention to yourself. You must glory in Christ and in Him alone (Alpha-Omega Ministries, Inc.).

My personal thoughts and feelings of inadequacies and the fear of using the voice that God gave me to proclaim, make known, and/or decree is absolutely irrelevant and in conflict to the purposes that God has ordained for me. If I choose to keep quiet but know the Word of God, I choose to preach to myself, and lift myself up. However, the ministry demands servitude; to be a servant to Jesus and to others. In other words, I am a slave to others by serving them and sharing the gospel of Jesus Christ. After all, Jesus sacrificed Himself for us and overcame the world for us, our sins, and to gain freedom for enslaving bondages (Alpha-Omega Ministries, Inc.).

Given that, desiring the Lord is to have the Lord's spirit and characteristics. The book of Galatians sums up nine attributes on living according to the Spirit, which are "love, joy, peace, longsuffering, gentleness, goodness, faith, meekness, and temperance" (Gal. 5:22-23). When we adopt the spirit of God, we acquire His virtue and excellency in our spiritual walk and in our mindset. We can then begin to walk by faith of what the Word of God says we are and not based on the opinions and the standards of who man says we are. The Holy Spirit produces one kind of fruit, and that is, Christ-likeness. Therefore, all of the fruits describe the life of a child of God. We all need love because God is the epitome of love when He demonstrated His love by giving His only begotten Son, Jesus Christ.

We have an instinctive ability to remain. We remain hurt, we remain comfortable, we remain in the same church, we remain in the same mindset and we remain fearful.

As brothers and sisters in Christ, peace is what creates harmony among us all. One sure thing is that we will have suffering in this world; long-suffering is patience in afflictions, annoyances, and persecutions. The suffering I endured is a testament of God's grace and of His love that lifted me when nothing else or no one else could help. Jesus teaches us through our sufferings that we must demonstrate kindness to one another, as His attitude toward His children. Walking by faith demonstrates our faithfulness to stand still to see the salvation of the Lord in the midst of difficulty. Self-discipline to trust God and to wait on Him to do the impossible can bring sentiments of anguish; however, it is important to show gentleness and self-control to help overcome temptations to demonstrate the fruits of the Spirit. All of these virtues are pleasing to God, beneficial to others, and good for ourselves as we live in communion with the Lord and become more like Him that we may better proclaim His gospel.

CHAPTER SIX

I have found that our immunity to change is a barrier to the benefits that God has in store for His children. As in the book, *Experiencing God,* it states that many people believed in God, served Him, and loved Him, but never experienced Him (Blackaby, Blackaby & King, 2021). We have an instinctive ability to remain. We remain hurt, we remain comfortable, we remain in the same church, we remain in the same mindset and we remain fearful. Although we mask the hurt, disappointment, fear, etc. by substituting other things like overindulging in church activities, becoming a workaholic, or taking our aggression out on others, we are still not growing and healing from past experiences. Holding on to the past hinders us from experiencing God and from seeing future aspects. Paul says in Philippians, "Not that I have already attained, or am already perfected; but I press on, that I may lay hold of that for which Christ Jesus has also laid hold of me … but one thing I do, forgetting those things which are behind and reaching forward to those things which are ahead ..." (Phil. 3:12-13). I am beginning to realize that satisfaction is the gravesite of growth. The process is on-going that we may attain grace to continue and deepen the work of God knowing that we may never be contented with our spiritual attainments. Some people that have riches, fine clothes and big houses may think that they have arrived and may be contented with material things. However, a man of single purpose "reaches towards every effort toward the goal for the prize of the upward call of God in Christ Jesus" (Phil. 3:14). The Apostle Paul is speaking to my spirit and soul when he expresses all the purposes God has in mind in saving us; our salvation, obedience in Christ, joint-heirship with Him, a home in heaven and blessings that we don't have room enough to receive. Yet, we must let go, let God and be willing to surrender so that change may occur.

In my inability to verbally communicate the disgraceful abuse that happened to me as a child, and also as an adult, it hindered my spiritual growth with God, as well as with my fellow brothers and sisters in Christ. Furthermore, I was holding back from sharing the gospel of Jesus Christ with non-believers or others that were struggling with their faith or acceptance of the Lord as their Savior. I allowed the fear and the shame that I felt to paralyze and to manipulate the power of my voice. Nevertheless, I learned that when we let go of our past mistakes and violations, and allow God to be ruler of our lives, we are able to be a living example of who He has ordained and called us to be. In accordant, John Dickson's statement implies that,

Downplaying the range of activities that promote Christ to the world has its own set of problems. It can make those who are not confident about speaking — of anything, let alone Jesus — feel inadequate and self-conscious in the task of reaching out to others. Equally, it can make those who do have a flair for speaking feel as though they are fulfilling Christ's mission just by talking. But the reality is that the Lord wants our whole life, not just our lips, in the task of bringing the gospel to the world. Every facet of our lives can be used by God to promote the news of his power and mercy (Dickson, John, 2010).

We can acquire the gift of God through the saving power of Jesus Christ. Professor De Kock does not differ in his statement that "the purpose is to make God's presence known when the knowledge of God is manifested." I have faith that in knowing God for myself, I may be known by God, and in that I must make God known to the world without fear, reservation, doubt, or hesitation. In doing so, it will help me to better proclaim the gospel. Prof. De Kock published that

The good news of Jesus Christ is to be proclaimed. We must announce, declare and herald, as in shout aloud the story of Jesus Christ according to the scripture. It is the complete story that Jesus was born fully in human conditions and not just for our sinfulness, but the fullness of our condition.

He died the death as our representative and as a substitutionary death, both physical and spiritual (eternal) death. His death procured forgiveness of sins, reconciliation with God, and justification before God's tribunal. In context, He died for our sins, He washed us in His blood, He sanctified and justified us, as the resolution and fulfillment of Israel's Story and promises (Wynand, De Kock, 2022).

Truly making a decision of whom I will serve is a pertinent decision that will transform my life to become more Christ-like that others may see the light of God within. It will become a testament of who He is, not just to me but to the world.

CHAPTER SEVEN

It is said that prayer is the key but faith unlocks the door (Psalm 102:11). We must believe that Christ died for us; for you and me. The wonderful thing about the Gospel is that objective justification manifests itself in subjective salvation. Jesus died for the entire world (I Jn. 2:2); therefore, He died for you, and thus, our sins are forgiven. A supportive likeness in Forde's book, *Theology is for Proclamation,* is of "two lovers conversing". He asks, "What would your girlfriend make of it when asking you if you love her? You answered yes, I love the whole world, or if you started talking about what love is, but never get around to proclaiming your love for her, exclusively." Similarly, we are commissioned to be God's spokesmen relating His love to those who have ears to hear what the Spirit of the Lord is saying to the church (Rev. 3:22); not just talk about God's love theoretically. We cannot give someone faith by talking about faith, but we give them something to believe in; that Jesus Christ died for the whole world. His contention ultimately is that our gospel proclamation should be more in line with the way the sacraments are administered; through His shed blood and His broken body. Our proclamation is to be that Christ died for us, with no room for discussion or debate. I believe that theology is to make the point that our sins are forgiven when Christ died for us; those who believe in Him. Forde endorses that it is true whether or not you believe it (Ford, Gerhard, 1990).

The question, why does seeking to win the approval of God, and not man important to proclaiming the gospel of Jesus Christ, mirrors the foundation of my personal theology that we must seek God's approval, instead of man's approval. God is the same yesterday, today and forever (Heb. 13:8) and He is the author and finisher of our faith (Heb. 12:2). He will never lead us wrong, but He will always guide our every footstep in the right direction. He is faithful to never fail us and His word is truth. With man, the flesh is weak; although the spirit may be willing. We are not always capable of doing the right thing even when we know right from wrong. In doing this, God will keep us focused on the assignment, and keep us humbled. For that reason, God's approval is the ultimate approval. He is the reason we live, move and have our being (Act 17:28). He is our source of strength, and our outlet. If we are not plugged into Him, we are powerless; however, we can do all things through Him who strengthens us (Phil. 4:13). His approval transcends any disapproval or isolation by man and it causes us to rise above every situation and circumstance with the absence of fear, phobias, or worry of what man can do. When God is for us, He is glorified, the sinner is mortified, and the saint is edified.

It is imperative for everyone to understand who God is, so that we may proclaim the true gospel of Jesus Christ without constraints. Putting our complete confidence in God and deciding whom we will serve is the general basis for us to grow in ministry and to serve the true and living God. God covers us under the shadow of His almighty wings and protects us throughout every storm in our lives that we may proclaim His goodness to all nations. The power of His resurrection and His love sustains us, as His power continually raises us, and sets us free.

We must decide whom we will serve; God not man. When we study His Word, we increase our knowledge of who God is that we may know Him and make Him known through our proclamation as we grow in His grace and as we diligently study His Word. It appears to be pretty simple; if we love Him, we will keep His commandments, right? However, free will is not always aligned to the Will of God. A man's heart is deceiving: but if we trust in the Lord, He will strengthen and lead us. As we apply the wisdom and knowledge of God to our lifestyle; which is the choice to make the decision to follow Him, it goes completely against what society deems as the normal way of life. The main objective that makes us apprehensive and uncomfortable as we work for the Kingdom, based on our own level of understanding and abilities, is the very thing that we should do.

As we are freed from disparities, such as abuse, neglect and boundaries, God enables us to use those hurtful conditions to press toward the healing of others that are suffering. Once I exposed the violations and used my voice to share with others how God raised me from despair to deliverance and victory, the enemy could no longer torture me with insults and manipulation.

We have limited power and authority, but God is all powerful and all knowing. He is able to empower us to rise above our mediocre thinking and doubts to impact the world through our short comings, mistakes and limited mindset. As we are freed from disparities, such as abuse, neglect and boundaries, God enables us to use those hurtful conditions to press toward the healing of others that are suffering. Once I exposed the violations and used my voice to share with others how God raised me from despair to deliverance and victory, the enemy could no longer torture me with insults and manipulation. God opened doors that allowed me to use my voice and share of how He turned my sorrow to joy and gave me beauty for ashes (Isa. 61:3). The more I studied and dedicated my life to God, the more spiritually confident I became. The more confident I became, the fear of others' judgment of me were diminished and replaced with boldness for the Lord. I didn't have to seek God for my assignments; His voice became clearer; therefore, His plans were ordering my steps as my gifts made room for me. Seeking God in prayer, studying His Word and acts of worship and service to others, has strengthen my heart and has shown me great and mighty things. God knocks at the door of our hearts and if we open, He will commune with us. There is absolutely no temptation that God just won't make a way of escape for us (I Cor. 10:13). Seeking God's approval is the only answer because He is God, the King of all kings and the Lord of all lords and to know Him is to love His Word.

PURPOSE

Webster's definition of purpose is, something set up as an object or end to be attained: Intention: Resolution, determination. A subject under discussion or an action in course of execution.

The biblical definition of purpose says it declares why we exist. It captures the heart of why you are on this earth and why Jesus died for us. It defines our lives, not in terms of what we think but what God thinks. It anchors our lives in the character and call of God. It clarifies the non-negotiables.

In reviewing the above definitions, I can place my life's purpose in the midst of them both. My purpose is an action towards a determination. I am determined to seek God that I may worship Him in spirit and in truth. It proclaims why I exist, captures the heart of why I am here on this earth, and why Jesus died for us. My sole purpose is to please God and not man. As God continues to call me deep unto deep, I will continue to fight the good fight of faith (by and through His grace) that I may hear Him one day say, come on up a little higher because I have been faithful among a few things. I am a living testimony; therefore, my pain was not just for my purpose, but for me to share with others to be uplifted, encouraged, and to have hope that God is able to do exceeding, abundantly above all we can ever think or imagine.

Our momentary light affliction is producing for us an eternal weight of glory far beyond comparison (NASB). For our present troubles are small and won't last very long. Yet they produce for us a glory that vastly outweighs them and will last forever (NLT) (2 Cor. 4:17). See, our affliction is light compared to what Jesus suffered for us. There is simply no comparison between what we are going through and all Jesus suffered spiritually, emotionally, and physically, all for us, not for Himself. Our affliction is light compared to the blessings we enjoy.

PAIN

The pain brought great discomfort, torment, low self-esteem, struggle and affliction. The most painful thing was losing me in the process of seeking love, and acceptance through people, and forgetting that I am special, too. The bible says to not put your confidence in man because they will fail you every time. As mentioned in my first book, I grew up in a loving home, but it was compromised when I was mistreated and abused by other family who were supposed to love me. There are wounds that never appear physically on the body that are deeper and profoundly more hurtful than anything that bleeds. It's also true that some wounds never heal completely, and begins to bleed again at the slightest of words, adding insult to injury. We can rest assured that God forgives when we go to Him and He can heal all of our sins and souls diseases. Until I wrote, *From Pain to Purpose,* I was walking in brokenness with a smile on my face; going through the motions and not understanding the internal sadness and pain. God called me to tell my story and He opened the doors to bless others by advocating as a volunteer with My Sister's House. His calling never stops; He pursues us and takes us deeper as we surrender to Him daily. He gave me a voice and through my pain, I am able to share with others His word through teaching biblical principles in various ministries at my church, Mount Moriah Missionary Baptist Church, and proclaiming the gospel of Jesus Christ of Nazareth. I am working out my salvation with fear and trembling while I trust God to do the impossible through this willing vessel. My pain is purposed for a desired outcome. The story continues as I live out my God-given purposes. There's no secret what God can do. What He's done for others, He will do the same for you.

THE PURPOSE FOR THE PAIN

We are troubled on every side, yet not distressed; we are perplexed, but not in despair; Persecuted, but not forsaken; cast down, but not destroyed; Always bearing about in the body the dying of the Lord Jesus, that the life also of Jesus might be made manifest in our body (2 Cor. 4: 8-10).

My heart, in all of its functions, was broken. The brokenness led me to know God for myself. If I had never been broken, I would have never known that He is a heart regulator; If I was never in lack, I would have never known that He is my provider; If I was never hungry, I would have never known Him to be my Bread of life and if I was never thirsty, I would not have never experienced His Living Water. Amen!

All of the intricacies of life that attack our hearts come to make us strong through seeking the Lord and becoming disciples for Him to gain the tools to overcome the assaults of the enemy. Seeking God and studying His word opened my heart to receive His provisions to pull me out of my darkness into His marvelous light. It gave me hope as I continued to press my way by standing on God's promises that He will never leave us nor will He forsake us, no weapon that is formed against us shall prosper, we are more than a conquerors in Christ Jesus, we are the head and not the tail, He will restore all that the enemy has stolen, His gifts will make room for us, and all these blessings will overtake us. Contrary to the quote, "too much of anything is not good for us", I stand on God's word in Psalm that says, "My soul follows hard after thee: thy right hand upholds me." Our purposes in life are definitely synonymous to how the heart functions; the fact is that everything centers on the matters of the heart, which is Jesus, our maker and creator. Drawing close to God will give us liberty to receive His healing, deliverance, and to be restored. In my despair, I was unable to see or understand my purpose; however, as I learned how to let go and let God; how to surrender my will for the will of the Father's; how to walk by faith and not by sight, the scales were removed from my eyes. Through trials that come and through heartache and pain, we will learn how to trust in Jesus and we learn how to trust in God that His word will not return unto Him void, His promises are true, He hears and answers prayers, He died to buy our pardon, He's a wheel in the middle of the wheel, and He ordained, sanctified and purposed us that we may prosper and be in health, etc. Everything that happens in life is only by and through the grace of God. God is our heart regulator. As I go forth, I hold fast to Joshua, who said to be bold, strong and courageous because our Lord God is with us wherever we go. Our purposes are in God to serve Him in spirit and in truth. We were created to worship Him and to be witnesses in the world. Growing close to Christ will open us to the attacks of the enemy, because He wants to kill and destroy us, but Jesus came that we may have life and have it more abundantly. But remember to guard your heart, as a good man out of the good treasure of his heart brings forth that which is good; and an evil man out of the evil treasure of his heart brings forth that which is evil: for out of the abundance of the heart, the mouth speaks (Luke 6:45). Simplified, what goes in will come out. Jesus reminds us that our speech and actions reveal our real, underlying beliefs, attitudes, and motivations. What is in your heart will come out in your speech and behavior. When we experience pain, suffering and disappointments, seek God for direction because behind every pain, is purpose. God is up to something and you can take Him at His word that He will never leave you alone and you were created for purpose. The bigger the pain, the bigger the praise; for it's in the valley that we grow. God's love never fails, and it never ends.

I will praise thee: for I am fearfully and wonderfully made: marvelous are thy works; and that my soul knows right well. Psalm 139:14

THE PURPOSE FOR THE PAIN

Poem by Rashad Taylor

I hate when it's quiet
When it's quiet, my thoughts become so loud, they tend to echo,
and memories start to crescendo and decrescendo crashing into one
another, leaving a mess to clean
Who's turn is it? Oh yeah it's mine, it's always mine.

You know, I really hate when it's quiet
Quiet reminds me that those conversations are over
The moment is gone
The present has just become the past, just like that
And then it's quiet

See, when it's quiet, there's no distraction, and
I'm forced to come to terms with conditions that
I didn't know I signed off on
Contractual agreements, my life is no longer mine

Understand when it's quiet
I'm confronted on if I'm a saint or a sinner
Inquired on if I'm for real or a pretender
Tested on if I'm a brake or bender

Surely there's a reason it gets quiet
I'm certain there will come a time where
I find solace in silence
But as for now, I just hate when it's quiet

JOURNEY REFLECTIONS

Sonja Pinckney Rhodes:

To me, her name covers a multitude of things, such as a friend, an advisor, Daughter, My Mom, Mother-in-Law, and Ya-Ya to her three grandchildren. As you read those names......what stands out to you? Do they stand out to you? No! Well, all of them stand out. Each one of those names tell a story, but do you know that story? Sonja Pinckney Rhodes, as you see

Mr. Jon Michael Pinckney, Sr.

today has been through many trials and tribulations that made her a valiant woman of God in all of those roles or categories that were listed. The ones you do not see are strength, diligent, caring, woman of God, Minister, leader, strong, counselor, etc.... There are so many that I can list, but I wouldn't have enough room. Did she start out this way.... NO, but through those trials and tribulations, her journey, test, and with God, she has grown to become the wonderful Woman of God you see today. Each day, she amazes me with how strong and how much she has grown. The way she walks, talks, and handles things is a true testament of what God has done in her life. She has been and is an inspiration to what you can do if you trust and believe in God.

Mr. Andre' Christoper Rhodes

Dear Momma,

Your purpose for the pain… When there is pain, there is always something to gain; Respect for yourself, Love for yourself, and Self-worth. It's the kind of pain that makes you see who you really are meant to be. There is no story like your story. When I see the motivation in you, I see it to be the greatness in you. The purpose for everything you do is out of love. The faith of God shines through you and your purpose for life is now your prime-time. I work hard to make you proud. There was no excuse for the pain, neither did you know the reason, but with your faith in God, you didn't doubt He would bring you through. The pain made you stronger, better, and more faithful. Now you know the Pain was for a Purpose.

Mrs. Sherri Pinckney Kinloch

Beautiful, intelligent, graceful, anointed and blessed are just a few of the adjectives that can be used to describe this woman of God!

To some, she's known as Jon and Andre's Mom, or Johnny and Mary Pinckney's oldest daughter, and while she's has been recognized over the years for all of those reasons, she is beginning to forge her own path, independent of those titles, and orchestrated by GOD.

I have been fortunate enough to witness her transformation from a young, high-spirited girl with the high-pitched voice, to a strong and mighty warrior and I love how GOD is using her for the HIS kingdom.

I am the youngest of our three siblings. Yes, Minister Sonja Rene Pinckney Rhodes is my big sis! There is nearly a five-year age difference between us, so at most points of our childhood it was difficult for us to relate to the others struggles, likes, and dislikes.

I was always a little on the "Tom-Boyish" side and Sonja was always very girlie. She was into fashion, make-up, dolls, etc. I on the other hand liked to play in the yard with the dog or ride my bike. Every once and a while, she would let her inner "Tomboy" reveal itself and climb the huge pine trees in our back yard with me or do cartwheels until we got dizzy. Some of my fondest memories were of us going on family trips to the beach, Disney World, or me, Sonja and our brother, Jonathan, spending our Summers at the YWCA on Coming Street.

We didn't develop a true friendship until our adult years, when we were able to understand the different life blessings and lessons that we faced. As a result, we have a beautiful bond not only as Sisters, but as friends and sisters in Christ.

I love who she is becoming, not just as a woman, but as a Minister and I pray that GOD will continue to elevate her and use her for HIS Glory and continues to pour into her as she exalts HIM and blesses her ministry to touch the lives of countless Men, Women, Boys and Girls.

"Now it will be, if you will diligently obey the voice of the Lord your God, being careful to do all His commandments which I am commanding you today, then the Lord your God will set you high above all the nations of the earth. 2 And all these blessings will come on you and overtake you if you listen to the voice of the Lord your God." MEV(Deuteronomy 28:1-2)

Mrs. Aleiya Pinckney Smalls

As I reflect over the past 6 months of my life ALL I CAN SAY IS, THANK YOU JESUS AND TO GOD BE THE GLORY FOR THE GREAT THINGS HE HAS TRULY DONE IN MY LIFE. I Thank God because as I am a living and walking Testimony. I thank God for life and for everything HE has done in the past, present and future. I'm truly grateful that I have been afforded a clean
slate and new perspective on life.

"O taste and see that the LORD is good: Blessed is the man that trusteth in him."
Psalm 34:8

To my Aunt Sonja Pinckney Rhodes, may God's grace continue to be upon you. You have been a confidant, teacher and advocator for many people. You're one that is always ready to serve and lend a helping hand. I pray your continued strength in the Lord. Continue to tell your story and be a voice to the unspoken and unheard. You have overcome many trials, tribulations and adversities that have molded you into a true God fearing virtuous woman. You're a living testimony to many who feel they may not have a voice. The Holy Spirit gave these words to me to repeat daily or weekly and now I want you to hold this near and dear to your heart.

You are.....

Beautiful	Amazing
Ecc. 3:11	Ps. 139:14
Victorious	Capable
Rom. 8:37	Mark 10:27
Enough	Chosen
2 Cor. 12:9	1 Thess. 1:4
Created	Never Alone
Gen. 1:31	Matt. 28:20
Strong	Always Loved
Phil. 4:13	Rom. 8:38

Mrs. Rebecca Bennett

What a Blessing God created, my beautiful niece, Sonja Pinckney Rhodes. I'm so proud of the woman that you have become, and all that you have accomplished. You spread love everywhere you go. Continue to be who you are and always put God first in your life. Keep striving for advancement, for you have great things ahead of you.

Let your light so shine before men that they may see your good works, and glorify your Father which is in heaven (Matthew 5:16).

Mrs. Nancy LaRoche

God doesn't uniquely position people into our lives without a profound purpose. Many may cross our paths, but only a few will continue life's journeys with you. I am so blessed that God chose Sonja Pinckney Rhodes to travel along with me through my personal navigation of life.

God placed Sonja into my life over 20 years ago through the Young Adult Choir Ministry at church where a spiritual spontaneous bonding was established. But, why? What was her purpose in my life? I didn't question God, but over the years He revealed the reasons. He knew I needed someone who would be loyal, dependable, honest, compassionate and most of all spiritual. That's Sonja!

He knew I needed someone I could share personal situations and struggles with. That's Sonja!

God knew I needed someone that if I called and there was silence on the phone....it was praying time. That's Sonja! God knew I needed someone who would pray for and with my children through their life's struggles. That's Sonja!

And finally, He knew I needed a spirit filled person to encourage and uplift me during dark times. That's Sonja!

These are just a few reasons why God uniquely positioned Sonja Pinckney Rhodes into my personal life. She has truly been a blessing and has been my "Bridge Over Troubled Waters".

Thank you God for revealing another one of her profound purposes.

I love you Sonja!

I can remember visiting my grandparents on their farm during summer break from school. As a young boy, I would often watch my grandmother plant seeds and then cover it with dirt. Then I would wait anxiously for something yummy to grow from that seed. Min. Sonja Pinckney Rhodes reminds me of those seeds; it has been a blessed, and inspiring journey to watch the seed that God has planted inside Sonja grow into something that not only inspires

Min. Tristan Simmons

others to overcome adversity, but also gives glory to God and sheds a light on the great things He can do for all of us. Her journey from pain to purpose, stands as a testimony to all that our tears and hurt from past, present, and future experiences can be used to cultivate, nourish and grow the seed that God has planted in all of us.

Chairman Dea. Thomas Withers

Minister Sonja Pinckney Rhodes has blossomed right before my very eyes. For more than 10 years we co-labored in the work of ministry at Mt. Moriah Missionary Baptist Church. I've watched a transformation take place in her life. She stands flat footed in acceptance of God's mission for her life. A once shy and reluctant soldier for God has risen through the ranks to become a dynamic speaker for those who've suffered hurt. Using her own life experiences and an indwelling of the Holy Spirit, Sonja has embraced the role of encourager, exalter, and foot soldier for God; a devoted Family member and friend. As she juggles several careers in retirement, Sonja maintains healthy and positive relationships with Family, friends and brothers and sisters in Christ, never passing up a chance to stop and lend a helping hand. Sonja projects a uniquely positive personality, all while navigating life's struggles of health challenges, single parenting, continuing education and loss of loved ones. She has held fast to her God and life goals. She works in ministry with expectation, purpose and an assuredness that through her the will of God will be accomplished. Her involvement and impact with various organizations and ministries in and around the city of Charleston, South Carolina, is exemplified by the countless awards and recognition she's received. Not too bad for a woman that experienced hurt and rejection early in life. But like a rose that sprang from the concrete, Minister Rhodes just keeps blossoming to display the beauty and strength God has placed inside of her.

Min. Dr. Nathalina Rogers-Tolbert

When you sent me the request to write a reflection for your book, I was honored. Then I inquired of the Lord of what does He want me to say. Then the lyrics of this song came to mind:

"Count on me through thick and thin
A friendship that will never end
When you are weak I will be strong
Helping you to carry on
Call on me, I will be there
Don't be afraid"

Quality friends are hard to find. But God blessed us and allowed us to meet and bond.

Even when Satan tried to sever the relationship through a misunderstanding and miscommunication, with time, prayer, Godly behaviors, and speaking love, the friendship was restored. During the awkwardness, I believe that God taught us much. Having hard conversations to get to the root of the problem taught us how to stay focused on solutions. It taught me the meaning of Proverbs 17:17 "A friend loves at all times and a brother is born for a time of adversity."

It was the spirit that helped us to persevere through the challenges. Yes, it was uncomfortable like the embryo of the seed breaking out of its coat. Just as the roots grew and fed off the soil, now we stand firm in faith because of the nutrients of Christ as the foundation of friendship. It was the pushing pass the pain to reach God's purpose that allowed us to grow closer together - from friends to sisters.

Psalm 133: 1 "Behold, how good and pleasant it is when brothers dwell in unity!"

Pushing pass the pain has allowed us to share painful experiences, especially how God heals the mind, body, and spirit. Through the process we have grown closer through the power of God & how He works things out for the good to those who love Him and are called according to His purposes. We are loved and we have purpose. We will continue to seek ye first the kingdom of God, and his righteousness; and all these things shall be added unto us (Matthew 6:33). We will continue to push pass the pain to reach our purpose. I love you my sister.

Dr. Lina

Dea. Archie Reid

God placed an open door before Sonja that no one can shut. In spite of her past history, Sonja's faith and trust in God has given her the strength to overcome hills and valleys in her life. Sonja has reached a pinnacle within herself that has allowed her to rise above adversity to see the beauty of what God has laid out for her. He knows the plan He has for her and Sonja is following the path less traveled and making her way through the ages with God as her Pilot. Sonja is a survivor and an overcomer. Although setbacks and disappointments are a part life, Sonja did not lose sight of the knowledge that Jesus is the author and finisher of her faith, allowing her to be who He really want her to be, a child of the King. The future is yours. Carpe Diem!

I have known Min. Sonja Pinckney Rhodes for over 10 years as we have labored together in various ministries in our local church. We originally met as brothers and sisters in Christ as members of Mt. Moriah Missionary Baptist Church. I quickly came to realize how gifted she was and her willingness to share those gifts with others through ministry. I have seen the

Dea. DeShean Garrett

seeds that were planted in her spirit produce good fruit through her works. She has been an inspiration to me and many others through her encouraging spirit and by her testimony; both in words and action. As she continued to mature in Christ, she has always been willing to go where God leads her, step out in faith, and use those gifts God has uniquely placed in her to help others.

Min. Rhodes was instrumental in re-establishing the Young Adult Ministry and continues to serve as an Advisor. I have seen the positive impact she has had in the lives of many young people in our Church. Min. Rhodes has also been an important part of growing the Young Adult Sunday School Ministry. I have personally witnessed how much she has grown in Christ through her sharing of God's Word with the Young Adults.

Min. Rhodes continues to share her testimony to encourage others that God is willing and able to see them through any trial, difficulty or setback.

What can I say about my friend, Sister-in-Christ, my cousin and Prayer Warrior...

Min. Sonja. Pinckney Rhodes, for as long as I have known her, has always had a beautiful, kind, and warm spirit. Her smile lights up any room she walks into. She is loved by so many people because of her genuine personality. She has a big

Min. Carmen Smalls Bowman

heart and is willing to share it with everyone she comes in contact with. God has called her and anointed her to serve in ministry, to share her story about purpose in the world of pain, and that is exactly what she has been doing.

Min. Rhodes is committed to the call of God on her life. She is a dedicated and faithful woman of God. Her children and grandchildren call her blessed. I am truly blessed to have her in my life as a friend, confidant, and prayer warrior. As a result of her surrender to the Lord, she boldly encourages other believers to walk in their inheritance and authority.

I pray this book will empower others to experience and attain peace and victory over the enemy.

In Jesus' name,

Min. Ranese Harrell

It's truly been a blessing and a gift from God when He placed Sonja Pinckney Rhodes into my life, of whom I refer to as a Spiritual daughter and leader. Witnessing her growth not only spiritually but within the community from the time of her first book until present has inspired my spiritual walk. Her writing has given me the encouragement I needed to finish this path and race of life.

Sonja truly demonstrates how a woman led by God will deny herself by being an inspiration to others through her life's testimony. Her light helps others learn how to release their fears, anxieties, and their past experiences through her spiritual walk and witness by trusting God no matter the age, level of circumstance, or educational background.

Sonja, my daughter in Christ, may you continue to grow and be a light to all who read your books and hear your stories.

ABOUT THE AUTHOR

Min. Sonja Pinckney Rhodes is a native Charlestonian raised in the West Ashley area by her loving parents, the late Dea. Johnny Pinckney and Mary Pinckney. She was born the second of three children and the oldest daughter. Sonja attended the public schools of Charleston County and in preparation for her career, earned her bachelor's degree in business management with a minor in human resources and a Master of Business Administration with a focus on human resource management. She is currently pursuing her Master of Theology degree from Palmer Theological Seminary/Eastern University.

Sonja is the proud mother of two sons, Jon Michael Pinckney, Sr., and Andre' Christopher Rhodes. She also delights in her lovely daughter-in-law, Markita Flemons Pinckney, and her three beautiful grandchildren, whom she adores, Jon Michael, Jr., Ari Samiya, and Nia Malika Pinckney.

Since May 2000, this woman of faith has been an active member of Mount Moriah Missionary Baptist Church, where the Rev. Dr. Byron L. Benton is her Senior Pastor. Here, she uses her gifts and talents to lead, inspire, and encourage. She serves as advisor to both the Young Adult Ministry and Baptist Young Women; she serves as a Sunday school teacher, co-facilitates the eLife Ministry; a member of CAJM-Charleston Area Justice Ministry and she is currently an Associate Minister of the gospel.

In June 2020, Sonja retired from the Medical University of South Carolina with nearly three decades of service, a life change where God has allowed her to focus on her purpose even more. She is an accomplished author with an international and two-time national number one best-selling books, *From Pain to Purpose: A Bridge Over Troubled Waters* and *Greater Works: A Compilation of Prayers for Everyday Life, 2nd edition*. In addition, Sonja is the founder and CEO of JMPinckney Publishing Company, LLC, a thriving real estate agent for Carolina Elite Realty, an official volunteer advocate and speaker for My Sister's House, a Charter Member of the International African American Museum and she was a Journalist for the former Historic Charleston Chronicle Newspaper. Moreover, she is the 2021 recipient of the House Resolution Award; the second highest award given to a South Carolinian by the House of Representatives for her life-time achievements and the 2021 recipient of the ACHI Women's Magazine Award for women who have achieved success in their chosen profession or career.

Whereas, Sonja has been able to accomplish many things, that at periods of time in her life seemed unattainable. Her goal is to help others heal so they can become all God has called them to be by moving from their pain to their purpose, which reflects one of her favorite scriptures that we can do all things through Christ who strengthens us. Philippians 4:13

NOTES

Alpha-Omega Ministries, Inc., 2017, What the Bible Says to the Minister, Pg. 131

Blackaby, Blackaby & King, (Experiencing God, 2021). Pg. 16

De Kock, Wynand, Eastern University.

Dickson, John, The Best Kept Secret of ChrisPan Mission: PromoPng the Gospel with More

ThanOur Lips. Grand Rapids, MI: Zondervan, 2010

Forde, Gerhard O. Theology is for ProclamaPon. Augsburg Fortress, 1990.

Franklin Roosevelt. Franklin Roosevelt. The White House. https://www.whitehouse.gov/about-the-white-house/presidents/franklin-d-roosevelt/#:~:text=Assuming%20the%20Presidency%20at%20the,to%20fear%20is%20fear%20itself.%E2%80%9D, n.d.

McKnight, Scot. 2016. "The King James Gospel." (Michigan: Zondervan, 2016). Pgs. 112 - 113

https://www.appleseeds.org/Deepest-Fear.htm.   August 18, 2022.

Wright, N.T. 1985. "Jesus, Israel and the Cross." Chico, CA: Scholars Press. P. 75-95.

Wright, N.T. 1995. "Romans and the Theology of Paul." Minneapolis: Fortress.

Made in the USA
Columbia, SC
04 June 2023

17494452R00058